# SHAKEN

NOT

# STIRRED

*101 Cocktails to make and enjoy!*

**DEDICATION**

# To the Boyners

All cocktails mixed by Johan, Fabrice and Georgio at LED

Farringdon Road London

Photography by Adam Lawrence

© 2000 by Parkgate Books Limited

This 2001 edition is published by Gramercy Books™,
an imprint of Random House Value Publishing. Inc.,
280 Park Avenue, New York, NY 10017.
by arrangement with Parkgate Books Limited,
London House, Great Eastern Wharf, Parkgate Road, London, SW11 4NQ

Gramercy Books™ and design are registered trademarks of
Random House Value Publishing

Random House
New York • Toronto • London • Sydney • Auckland
http://www.randomhouse.com/

A CIP catalogue record for this book is available from the Library of Congress

ISBN 0-517-16320-9

Printed and Bound in China

8 7 6 5 4 3 2 1

# SHAKEN
### NOT
# STIRRED

*101 Cocktails to make and enjoy!*

## Compiled by Paul Effeny

GRAMERCY

# Contents

# SHAKEN NOT STIRRED

The Cocktails:

1 Acapulco
2 Alabama Slammer
3 Around the World
4 B-52
5 Bellini
6 Between the Sheets
7 Bikini
8 Black Russian
9 Black Velvet
10 Blood and Sand
11 Bloody Mary
12 Blue Hawaiian
13 Blue Lagoon
14 Brandy Alexander
15 Brown Cow
16 Caipirinha
17 Casablanca
18 Champagne Cocktail
19 Clover Club
20 Cosmopolitan
21 Cuba Libre
22 Daiquiri
23 Damn the Weather
24 Dunk
25 Fluffy Duck
26 Fool's Gold
27 Fuzzy Navel
28 Gilroy
29 Gimlet
30 Gloom Chaser
31 Golden Dream
32 Grasshopper
33 Green Dragon
34 Harvey Wallbanger
35 Hawaiian
36 Honeymoon
37 Hummer
38 Hurricane
39 Income Tax
40 Indian Summer
41 Irish Coffee
42 Jack Rose
43 Jelly Bean
44 John Collins
45 Kamikaze
46 Kir Royale
47 Kiss Me Quick
48 Long Island Iced Tea
49 Los Angeles
50 Lynchberg Lemonade
51 Madam I'm Adam
52 Mai Tai

53 Manhattan
54 Margarita
55 Martini (dry)
56 Metropolitan
57 Millionaire
58 Mimosa
59 Mind Your Razor
60 Mint Julep
61 Mojito
62 Morning Glory
63 Moscow Mule
64 Nineteenth Hole, The
65 Old-Fashioned
66 Paradise
67 Perfect Love
68 Pimms No 1
69 Piña Colada
70 Pink Gin
71 Pink Panther
72 Red Baron
73 Red Lion
74 Rob Roy
75 Rose
76 Rusty Nail
77 Salty Dog
78 Save the Planet
79 Scarlett O'Hara
80 Scorpion
81 Screwdriver
82 Sea Breeze
83 Sex on the Beach
84 Side Car
85 Singapore Sling
86 Sloe Comfortable
   Screw against the
   Wall - with a Kiss
87 Snowball
88 Southern Frappé
89 Stinger
90 Tequila Sunrise
91 Top Banana
92 Venetian Lagoon
93 Whiskey Sour
94 Whiskey Toddy
95 Zombie

The Shooters:

96 After Eight
97 Grandpa is Alive
98 Jamaican Slammer
99 Red, White and Blue
100 Spider Bite
101 Thin Blue Line

# Cocktail
# Creation

Cocktails are refined. Cocktails are indulgent. Cocktails are fun. You can make classic cocktails, or weird hybrids. There are no rules. Experiment with different spirits and colors, enjoy them, name them and share them with your friends, but remember just how potent they can be: the average short cocktail contains the same amount of alcohol as three glasses of wine...

the tumbler

the highball

the goblet

the flute

the cocktail glass

the mug

# Bartender's Notes

The cocktails in this book can all be made following simple measurements and instructions. The notes below explain the various terms.

A **bar glass:** a tall jug with no handle equipped with a glass stirring rod or long handled spoon.

**Bitters:** are made from herbs and/or fruit. There are four kinds, the most common being Angostura and orange.

To **blend:** pour the ingredients into a blender, and mix. Don't overdo it, but drinks with fruit or ice cream in will need longer.

To **chill** a glass: either refrigerate in advance or fill with ice and club soda for a couple of minutes. Discard the mixture, pour the cocktail. Cocktails made in highball and tumbler glasses usually contain their own ice, but cocktails made in cocktail glasses, goblets and flutes do not, thus the glass should be chilled. The stems of these glasses mean that the hand holding the glass does not warm up the contents.

To **coat** a glass: swill the liquid around the empty glass, throwing away the excess.

**To make cracked ice:** take the ice cubes, wrap them in a cloth and hit them a few times with a rolling pin.

A **dash** is a quick spurt that comes from a bottle, such as Worcestershire sauce or Angostura bitters.

To get an exact **drop:** try dipping the end of a straw into the liquid and closing the other end with your finger.

To **float:** hold a teaspoon upside-down as close as you can to the surface of the cocktail. Pour the liquid gently on to the back of the teaspoon .

**Frosting:** pour some salt or sugar into a saucer, wipe the rim of the glass with a fruit juice or egg white, and dip the rim into the saucer. You can add food coloring to the

salt or sugar to add a little glamour.

To make **froth:** as for shaking, but shake until the liquid and the cracked ice has combined to make froth. Don't shake drinks with carbonated ingredients!

To **shake:** using a cocktail shaker, pour in the ingredients, usually with cracked ice, and shake vigorously until the outside of the shaker is frosty. There are two kinds of shaker: the traditional kind in which ice and ingredients mix, and a more modern kind in which the ice is kept separate from the ingredients to stop them diluting. Mixtures from both kinds still need to be strained.

One **shot** or measure is 25ml, or just under 1oz.

To **stir:** pour the ingredients into a bar glass, and using a long-handled teaspoon or glass rod, stir together. Stir carbonated drinks gently, and always stir

drinks that include ice and clear liqueurs.

A **stirrer:** a long handled teaspoon or a glass stirring rod.

To make a pint of **sugar syrup** (also known as gomme): dissolve one pound (450g) of granulated sugar in half a pint (300ml) of hot water. Stir slowly, and add another half a pint (300ml) of cold water.

Many cocktails include a dash of lime, a dash

of lemon and a dash of sugar syrup; this is a **'sweet and sour mix'**. If you are having a cocktail party, it's a good idea to make up a glassful of this before you start.

To **strain:** this is not only to remove the ice, but also any bits of fruit, thus ensuring a smooth cocktail. You can buy a cocktail strainer, but a tea strainer will do.

# Garnishes

There are few rules about garnishes. As long as your garnish is sympathetic to your cocktail, enjoy free expression. However, cocktails are all about appearances; you don't have to eat a garnish, but it does have to look inviting.

Don't overdo it: a multitude of straws, umbrellas, flowers and colored ice cubes can be fun, but in most cases, less is more and a single twist of lemon peel, a cherry or an olive can be most effective.

Apple, cherries, kiwi fruit, lemon, lime, melon, orange, pineapple, strawberry, cucumber and mint are all most acceptable. Use any fruit that you think will complement the base elements of your creation.

To make a *twist:* using a zester, pare off a length of peel, avoiding the pith. Tie a knot in it, and add to cocktail.

To make a *curly twist:* wrap the twist around a straw. Take it off and add to cocktail. Bending or knotting the twist releases flavored oils held in the rind.

Cherries can either float in the cocktail, or you can pierce them with a cocktail stick, and wedge them on the rim of the glass, having cut a notch in the base of the cherry.

To make a *wheel:* take a citrus fruit, and use the zester to score the skin from top to bottom, making eight divisions. When the fruit is sliced, each slice is a wheel.

# The
# Cocktails

# Acapulco

**Glass:** highball

**Ingredients:**
- one shot of white rum
- one shot of tequila
- pineapple juice
- grapefruit juice

**Method**
Pour the rum and tequila over ice. Top up with equal measures of pineapple and grapefruit juice.

# Alabama Slammer

**Glass:** tumbler

**Ingredients:**
- one shot of whiskey
- one shot of sloe gin
- one shot of triple sec
- one shot of Galliano
- orange juice

**Method**
Shake the whiskey, gin, triple sec and Galliano with cracked ice. Strain, and pour. Top up with orange juice.

**Garnish:** a cherry and a slice of orange

# Around the World

**Glass:** highball

**Ingredients:**
- one and a half shots of gin
- one and a half shots of green Crème de Menthe
- two/three shots of pineapple juice

**Method**
Shake all the ingredients with cracked ice. Strain and pour over ice.

**Garnish:** a sprig of mint

# B-52

**Glass:** highball

**Ingredients:**
- one shot of Bailey's Irish Cream
- one shot of Kahlua
- one shot of Grand Marnier

**Method**
Shake all the ingredients with cracked ice. Strain, and pour over ice.

# Bellini

**Glass:** flute

**Ingredients:**
- half a shot of peach schnapps
- champagne

**Method**
First pour the peach schnapps, then top up with the champagne.

# Between the Sheets

**Glass:** cocktail

**Ingredients:**
- two-thirds of a shot of brandy
- two-thirds of a shot of white rum
- two-thirds of a shot of triple sec
- a dash of lemon juice

**Method**
Shake all the ingredients with cracked ice. Strain and pour.

**Garnish:** a lemon twist

# Bikini

**Glass:** cocktail

**Ingredients:**
- one and a half shots of vodka
- half a shot of white rum
- a dash of lemon juice
- a dash of milk
- a dash of sugar syrup

**Method**
Shake all the ingredients with cracked ice. Strain and pour.

**Garnish:** a lemon wheel

# Black Russian

**Glass:** highball

**Ingredients:**
- two shots of vodka
- one shot of Kahlua
- cola

**Method**
Shake the vodka and Kahlua with cracked ice. Strain and pour over ice. Top up with cola.

If this is made with cream instead of cola, it's a White Russian.

Or with Tia Maria instead of Kahlua, then it's a Black Cloud.

# Black Velvet

**Glass:** goblet

**Ingredients:**
- Guinness
- champagne

**Method**
Pour equal measures of the ingredients, Guinness first, into a glass. Stir gently.

# Blood and Sand

**Glass:** cocktail

**Ingredients:**
- one shot of whiskey
- half a shot of cherry brandy
- half a shot of sweet vermouth
- a shot of orange juice

**Method**
Shake all the ingredients with cracked ice. Strain and pour.

**Garnish:** a slice of orange

**Glass:** tumbler

**Ingredients:**
- two shots of vodka
- one shot of lemon juice
- a dash of dry sherry (optional)
- four shots of tomato juice
- one teaspoon of horseradish sauce
- a teaspoon of Worcester sauce
- half a teaspoon of Tabasco
- a pinch of salt
- a pinch of pepper

**Method**
Mix all the ingredients in a blender, and pour over ice.

**Garnish:** a stick of celery and a lemon wheel

The classic hangover cure.

If this is made as a non-alcoholic cocktail, without the vodka, it's called a Virgin Mary.

# Bloody Mary

# Blue Hawaiian

**Glass:** goblet

**Ingredients:**
- one shot of light rum
- one shot of blue Curaçao
- one shot of cream of coconut
- two shots of pineapple juice

**Method**
Shake all the ingredients with cracked ice. Strain, and pour.

**Garnish:** a wedge of orange

# Blue Lagoon

**Glass:** tumbler

**Ingredients:**
- one and a half shots of vodka
- half a shot of blue Curaçao
- four shots of pineapple juice

**Method**
Stir all the ingredients together in a bar glass. Pour over ice. Gently pour a dash of blue Curaçao over the top.

**Garnish:** slices of orange or pineapple

# Brandy Alexander

**Glass:** cocktail

**Ingredients:**
- one and half shots of brandy
- half a shot of white Crème de Cacao
- one shot of cream

**Method**
Shake all the ingredients with cracked ice. Strain and pour.

**Garnish:** grated nutmeg

# Brown Cow

**Glass:** cocktail

**Ingredients:**
- two shots of Kahlua
- one shot of cream

**Method**
Shake the ingredients with cracked ice. Strain and pour.

**Garnish:** a cherry

This can be made as a long drink, in a tumbler, with one shot of Kahlua and four shots of milk.

# Caipirinha

**Glass:** highball

**Ingredients:**
- one lime, cut into eight segments
- two shots of Cachaça
- a dash of lime juice
- a soup spoon of sugar

**Method**
Mix the lime, lime juice and sugar until the sugar is dissolved. Add ice, then the Cachaça.

# Casablanca

**Glass:** cocktail

**Ingredients:**
- one and a half shots of white rum
- half a shot of cherry liqueur
- half a shot of triple sec
- half a shot of lime juice

**Method**
Shake all the ingredients with cracked ice. Strain and pour.

**Garnish:** a lime wheel and lime and orange twists

# Champagne Cocktail

**Glass:** flute

**Ingredients:**
- a sugar cube
- a dash of bitters
- one shot of brandy
- champagne
- half a shot of Grand Marnier

**Method**
Put the sugar cube in the glass, and add the bitters, then the brandy, then top up with champagne. Lastly, float the Grand Marnier on top.

**Glass:** cocktail

**Ingredients:**
- one and a half shots of gin
- half a shot of grenadine
- half a shot of lemon juice
- one egg white

**Method**
Shake all the ingredients with cracked ice. Strain and pour.

# Clover Club

# Cosmopolitan

**Glass:** cocktail

**Ingredients:**
- one shot of Cointreau
- one shot of lemon vodka (Absolut Citron)
- half a shot of lime juice
- a dash of cranberry juice

**Method**
Shake all the ingredients with cracked ice. Strain and pour.

**Garnish:** a twist of lime

**Glass:** tumbler

**Ingredients:**
- two shots of white rum
- half a shot of lime juice
- cola

**Method**
Pour the rum and lime juice over ice. Top up with cola.

**Garnish:** a twist and a wedge of lime

# Cuba Libre

**Glass:** tumbler

**Ingredients:**
- three shots of light rum
- one shot of lemon juice
- one shot of lime juice
- a dash of sugar syrup

**Method**
Shake all the ingredients with cracked ice. Strain and pour over ice.

**Garnish:** a lime wheel

# Daiquiri

# Damn the Weather

**Glass:** cocktail

**Ingredients:**
- one and a half shots of gin
- half a shot of sweet vermouth
- a dash of triple sec
- one shot of orange juice

**Method**
Shake all the ingredients with cracked ice. Strain and pour.

**Garnish:** an orange twist

# Dunk

**Glass:** cocktail

**Ingredients:**
- one and a half shots of gin
- half a shot of Galliano
- half a shot of blue Curaçao

**Method**
Stir the ingredients in a bar glass, and pour.

**Garnish:** an orange twist

# Fluffy Duck

**Glass:** highball

**Ingredients:**
- one shot of Bacardi
- one shot of Advocaat
  (a Dutch eggnog)
- Sprite or 7up
- cream

**Method**
Pour the Bacardi and
Advocaat onto ice. Top up
with Sprite or 7up, and pour
a float of cream on top.

**Garnish:** a strawberry fan
(half slice a strawberry
several times, and fan it out
a little)

This is a favorite among
those with a less robust
approach to alcohol.

# Fool's Gold

**Glass:** tumbler

**Ingredients:**
- one shot of gold tequila
- one shot of triple sec
- a dash of lime juice
- a dash of lemon juice
- a dash of sugar syrup
- five drops of Tabasco
- cola

**Method**
Shake everything except the
cola and the Tobasco with
cracked ice. Strain and pour
over ice. Top up with cola
and add the Tobasco.

**Garnish:** a lemon wheel

# Fuzzy Navel

**Glass:** highball

**Ingredients:**
- two shots of peach schnapps
- orange juice

**Method**
Pour the peach schnapps over ice. Top up with orange juice.

**Garnish:** slices of orange

**Glass:** cocktail

**Ingredients:**
- one shot of gin
- one shot of cherry brandy
- half a shot of dry vermouth
- half a shot of lemon juice
- a dash of bitters

**Method**
Shake all the ingredients with cracked ice. Strain and pour.

**Garnish:** a cherry and an orange twist

# Gilroy

# Gimlet

**Glass:** cocktail

**Ingredients:**
- one and a half shots of gin
- half a shot of lime cordial or lime juice
- club soda

**Method**
Stir the gin and lime cordial together and pour into glass. Top up with club soda.

**Garnish:** a slice of lemon or lime

This can also be made with vodka instead of gin.

**Glass:** cocktail

**Ingredients:**
- one shot of orange Curaçao
- one shot of Grand Marnier
- one shot of lemon juice
- a dash of grenadine

**Method**
Shake all the ingredients with cracked ice. Strain and pour.

**Garnish:** lemon and lime twists

# Gloom Chaser

# Golden Dream

**Glass:** tumbler

**Ingredients:**
- two shots of Cointreau
- a dash of Galliano
- a dash of cream
- four shots of orange juice

**Method**
Shake all the ingredients with cracked ice. Strain and pour.

**Garnish:** a slice of orange and a cherry

This can be made as a short cocktail, with one shot of Galliano, half a shot of Cointreau, half a shot of orange juice and half a shot of cream.

**Glass:** cocktail

**Ingredients:**
- one shot of white Crème de Cacao
- one shot of green Crème de Menthe
- one shot of cream

**Method**
Shake all the ingredients with cracked ice. Strain and pour.

**Garnish:** a cherry

If this is made with vodka instead of cream, it's a Flying Grasshopper.

# Grasshopper

32

**Glass:** cocktail

**Ingredients:**
- two shots of vodka
- one shot of Green Chartreuse

**Method**
Shake all the ingredients with cracked ice. Strain and pour.

**Garnish:** a cherry

# Green Dragon

# Harvey Wallbanger

**Glass:** tumbler

**Ingredients:**
- one and a half shots of vodka
- half a shot of Galliano
- orange juice

**Method**
Pour the vodka and Galliano over ice. Top up with orange juice and stir.

**Garnish:** slices of orange.

If this is made with tequila instead of vodka it's a Freddy Fudpucker.

# Hawaiian

**Glass:** cocktail

**Ingredients:**
- two shots of gin
- half a shot of triple sec
- half a shot of pineapple juice

**Method**
Shake all the ingredients with cracked ice. Strain and pour.

**Garnish:** cherries and an orange wheel

**Glass:** cocktail

**Ingredients:**
- one shot of Benedictine
- one shot of Calvados
- half a shot of triple sec
- half a shot of lemon juice

**Method**
Shake all the ingredients with cracked ice. Strain and pour.

**Garnish:** a slice of lemon and a lemon twist

# Honeymoon

# Hummer

**Glass:** tumbler

**Ingredients:**
- one shot of light rum
- one shot of Tia Maria
- two scoops of vanilla ice-cream

**Method**
Briefly blend the ingredients, and pour over ice.

**Garnish:** grate some nutmeg over the top

**Glass:** tumbler

**Ingredients:**
- one and a half shots of dark rum
- one and a half shots of white rum
- one shot of gin
- half a shot of Amaretto
- a dash of grenadine
- orange juice
- grapefruit juice
- pineapple juice

**Method**
Mix all the ingredients in a bar glass and pour over ice. Top up with equal measure of the fruit juices.

**Garnish:** a cherry and a lime wedge

If this is made as a non-alcoholic cocktail, without the rum, gin and Amaretto, adding a dash of Angostura bitters and some sugar syrup, it is called a Zephyr. (Put the grenadine in first.)

# Hurricane

# Income Tax

**Glass:** highball

**Ingredients:**
- two shots of gin
- half a shot of dry vermouth
- half a shot of sweet vermouth
- one shot of orange
- two or three dashes of bitters

**Method**
Shake all the ingredients with cracked ice. Strain and pour over ice.

**Garnish:** a slice of orange

# Indian Summer

**Glass:** highball

**Ingredients:**
- one shot of vodka
- one shot of Kahlua
- two shots of pineapple juice

**Method**
Shake all the ingredients with cracked ice. Strain and pour over ice.

**Glass:** goblet or mug

**Ingredients:**
- one and a half shots of Irish Whiskey
- one and a half teaspoons of sugar
- black coffee
- whipped cream

**Method**
Put the whiskey in the glass, add the sugar and fill with coffee. Stir. Float the whipped cream on top.

# Irish Coffee

# Jack Rose

**Glass:** cocktail

**Ingredients:**
- two shots of Calvados
- half a shot of grenadine
- half a shot of lemon juice

**Method**
Shake all the ingredients with cracked ice. Strain and pour.

**Garnish:** a lime twist

# Jelly Bean

**Glass:** tumbler

**Ingredients:**
- one shot of blue Curaçao
- one shot of grenadine
- two shots of ouzo
- Sprite or 7up

**Method**
Pour the Curaçao, grenadine and ouzo over ice. Stir and top up with Sprite or 7up.

**Garnish:** slices of orange and lime

**Glass:** tumbler

**Ingredients:**
- two shots of whiskey
- one shot of lemon juice
- a dash of sugar syrup
- club soda

**Method**
Shake the whiskey, lemon juice and sugar syrup with cracked ice. Strain and pour over ice. Top up with club soda and stir gently.

**Garnish:** a cherry and slices of orange and lemon

If made with gin, this is a Tom Collins.

# John Collins

# Kamikaze

**Glass:** tumbler

**Ingredients:**
- one and a half shots of vodka
- one and a half shots of triple sec
- one shot of lime juice
- one shot of lemon juice

**Method**
Shake all the ingredients with cracked ice. Strain and pour over ice.

**Garnish:** a wedge and a twist of lime

**Glass:** flute

**Ingredients:**
- a dash of Crème de Cassis
- champagne

**Method**
Put the Crème de Cassis in the bottom of the flute, and top up with champagne.

This is a great way to disguise and liven up cheap fizz!

If it is made with white wine instead of champagne, it's called Kir.

# Kir Royale

# Kiss Me Quick

**Glass:** tumbler

**Ingredients:**
- two shots of Pernod
- a teaspoon of triple sec
- five drops of Angostura bitters
- club soda

**Method**
Shake the Pernod, triple sec and bitters with cracked ice. Strain and pour over ice. Top up with club soda.

**Garnish:** a twist and a slice of orange

# Long Island Iced Tea

**Glass:** tumbler

**Ingredients:**
- one shot of vodka
- half a shot of gin
- half a shot of triple sec
- half a shot of white rum
- half a shot of tequila
- quarter of a shot of lime juice
- quarter of a shot of lemon juice
- a dash of sugar syrup
- cola

**Method**
Mix everything except the cola in a bar glass. Pour over ice and top up with cola.

**Garnish:** slices of lemon

If this is made with cranberry juice instead of cola, it's a Long Beach Iced Tea.

# Los Angeles

**Glass:** goblet

**Ingredients:**
- two shots of whiskey
- a dash of sweet vermouth
- one shot of lemon
- a teaspoon of sugar syrup
- one egg

**Method**
Shake all the ingredients with cracked ice. Strain and pour.

**Garnish:** a lemon twist

# Lynchberg Lemonade

**Glass:** highball

**Ingredients:**
- one shot of Jack Daniels whiskey
- one shot of triple sec
- half a shot of lemon juice
- Sprite or 7up

**Method**
Pour the whiskey, triple sec and lemon juice over ice. Stir and top up with Sprite or 7up.

**Garnish:** a twist and a slice of lemon

**Glass:** goblet

**Ingredients:**
- one shot of vodka
- a dash of triple sec
- one shot of cranberry juice
- one shot of grapefruit juice

**for the froth:**
- half a shot of pineapple juice

**Method**
Shake the vodka, triple sec and cranberry juice with cracked ice. Strain and pour. Add the grapefruit juice. Next shake half a shot of pineapple juice with cracked ice until a froth is formed, and spoon it over the top.

**Garnish:** lime peel and a strawberry

This can be made as a non-alcoholic cocktail, leaving out the vodka and triple sec and adding a shot of orange juice.

# Madam I'm Adam

# Mai Tai

**Glass:** tumbler

**Ingredients:**
- one shot of light rum
- one shot of dark rum
- half a shot of orange Curaçao
- half a shot of apricot brandy
- half a shot of Amaretto (optional)
- half a shot of lime juice
- pineapple juice

**Method**
Mix everything except the pineapple juice in a bar glass and pour over ice. Top up with pineapple juice.

**Garnish:** an orange twist

# Manhattan

# Margarita

**Glass:** cocktail

**Ingredients:**
- one shot of tequila
- one shot of triple sec
- one shot of lime juice

**Method**
Frost the rim of the glass with salt. Shake all the ingredients with cracked ice. Strain and pour.

**Glass:** cocktail

**Ingredients:**
- one shot of whiskey (rye whiskey if possible)
- half a shot of sweet vermouth
- half a shot of dry vermouth
- a dash of Angostura bitters

**Method**
Coat the glass with Angostura bitters. Stir the whiskey, and both vermouths in a bar glass with cracked ice. Strain, and pour.

**Garnish:** cherries

Reputedly the original cocktail.

# Martini (dry)

**Glass:** cocktail

**Ingredients:**
- one and a half shots of vodka
- half a shot of dry vermouth

**Method**
Shake the ingredients with cracked ice. Strain and pour.

**Garnish:** olives

A medium martini is as above, with an extra half shot of sweet vermouth.

A sweet martini has only sweet vermouth and vodka.

Varying degrees of dryness can be achieved by decreasing the dry vermouth; some people merely coat the glass with it.

Martinis can also be made with gin.

# Metropolitan

**Glass:** cocktail

**Ingredients:**
- two shots of brandy
- one shot of sweet vermouth
- a dash of Angostura bitters

**Method**
Coat the glass with the bitters. Shake the brandy and vermouth with cracked ice. Strain and pour.

**Garnish:** a cherry

# Millionaire

**Glass:** cocktail

**Ingredients:**
- one and a half shots of whiskey (preferably bourbon)
- one shot of Pernod
- a dash of triple sec
- a dash of grenadine
- one egg white

**Method**
Shake all the ingredients with cracked ice. Strain and pour.

**Garnish:** slices of orange

# Mimosa

**Glass:** flute

**Ingredients:**
- a dash of orange Curaçao
- one shot of orange juice
- champagne

**Method**
First pour the orange juice, then add the Curaçao. Top up with champagne.

To make Buck's Fizz, combine one-third of orange juice to two-thirds of champagne.

To make this as a non-alcoholic cocktail, Ginger Fizz, mix equal measures of orange juice and ginger ale.

# Mind Your Razor

**Glass:** goblet

**Ingredients:**
- one shot of Kahlua
- one shot of vodka
- club soda

**Method**
Pour the Kahlua, then the vodka. Top up with club soda.

# Mint Julep

# Mojito

**Glass:** tumbler

**Ingredients:**
- two shots of white or dark rum
- one shot of lime juice
- one teaspoon of brown sugar
- ten leaves of fresh mint
- club soda

**Method**
Mash the mint and sugar together. Add the rum and lime juice and pour over ice. Top up with club soda.

**Garnish:** lime wheels and a sprig of mint

To make this as a non-alcoholic cocktail, leave out the rum. It is a refreshing summer cooler.

**Glass:** tumbler

**Ingredients:**
- three shots of bourbon
- one teaspoon of brown sugar
- ten leaves of fresh mint
- half a teaspoon of water

**Method**
Mash the mint and sugar with half a teaspoon of water. Put the mixture in the glass and add lots of cracked ice. Pour the bourbon over and stir until the glass frosts.

**Glass:** tumbler

**Ingredients:**
- one and a half shots of brandy
- three-quarters of a shot of orange Curaçao
- two dashes of Angostura bitters
- two dashes of Pernod
- three-quarters of a shot of lemon juice
- a teaspoon of sugar syrup
- club soda

**Method**
Shake everything except the club soda with cracked ice. Strain and pour. Top up with club soda.

**Garnish:** an orange slice, a lemon twist and a cherry

# Morning Glory

# Moscow Mule

**Glass:** tumbler

**Ingredients:**
- two shots of vodka
- one shot of lime juice
- a dash of Angostura bitters
- ginger beer

**Method**
Mix the vodka, lime and bitters together in a bar glass and pour over ice. Top up with ginger beer and stir gently.

**Garnish:** a slice of lime

# The Nineteenth Hole

**Glass:** tumbler

**Ingredients:**
- one shot of Campari
- three shots of lemon soda (or old-fashioned lemonade and fresh lime juice)
- two shots of melon liqueur (Midori)

**Method**
Pour the lemon soda over ice, adding the Campari down the inside of the glass. Top up with the melon liqueur.

**Garnish:** a lime dinghy, with a small cargo of Campari

# Old-Fashioned

**Glass:** highball

**Ingredients:**
- two shots of bourbon
- two dashes of bitters
- a ground-up sugar cube

**Method**
Mix the sugar and bitters until the sugar dissolves. Add some ice cubes, then pour over the whiskey.

**Garnish:** cherries and a lemon twist

# Paradise

**Glass:** cocktail

**Ingredients:**
- one shot of gin
- one shot of apricot brandy
- one shot of orange juice

**Method**
Shake all the ingredients with cracked ice. Strain and pour.

**Garnish:** cherries and a wedge of orange

67

# Perfect Love

**Glass:** highball

**Ingredients:**
- two shots of vodka
- one shot of Liqueur
- one shot of Maraschino

**Method**
Pour the ingredients, in this order, over ice.

**Garnish:** a twist of lemon peel

# Pimms No 1

**Glass:** tumbler

**Ingredients:**
- two shots of Pimms No 1
- Sprite or 7up
- sliced cucumber
- chopped fruit (e.g. orange, pineapple, banana, apple)

**Method**
Pour the Pimms over the fruit and ice. Top up with Sprite or 7up.

**Garnish:** slices of orange, lime, mint and cucumber

This can also be made with Pimms No 2, which is vodka, rather than gin-based.

**Glass:** tumbler

**Ingredients:**
- two shots of gold rum
- one teaspoon of cream of coconut
- three shots of pineapple juice
- a dash of cream

**Method**
Mix all of the ingredients in a blender until smooth. Pour over ice.

**Garnish:** a slice of orange and an orange fan

To make this as a non-alcoholic cocktail, leave out the rum and add a dash of bitters.

# Piña Colada

# Pink Gin

**Glass:** highball

**Ingredients:**
- one shot of gin
- one shot of water
- 3 dashes of Angostura bitters

**Method**
Pour the gin over ice, then the water, then add the bitters.

# Pink Panther

**Glass:** cocktail

**Ingredients:**
- three-quarters of a shot of gin
- three-quarters of a shot of dry vermouth
- half a shot of Crème de Cassis
- half a shot of orange juice
- one egg white

**Method**
Shake all the ingredients with cracked ice. Strain and pour.

**Garnish:** strips of orange peel

# Red Baron

**Glass:** cocktail

**Ingredients:**
- two shots of gin
- half a shot of orange juice
- a dash of grenadine
- a dash of lemon juice
- a dash of lime juice
- a dash of sugar syrup

**Method**
Shake all the ingredients with cracked ice. Strain and pour.

**Garnish:** a twist of orange

# Red Lion

**Glass:** goblet

**Ingredients:**
- two shots of Grand Marnier
- one shot of gin
- one shot of lemon juice
- one shot of orange juice

**Method**
Frost the rim of the glass with sugar. Shake all the ingredients with cracked ice. Strain and pour.

# Rob Roy

**Glass:** cocktail

**Ingredients:**
- a dash of Angostura bitters
- one and a half shots of whiskey
- one shot of sweet vermouth

**Method**
Coat the glass with the bitters. Shake the whiskey and vermouth with cracked ice. Strain and pour.

**Garnish:** cherries and a lemon twist

# Rose

**Glass:** cocktail

**Ingredients:**
- one and a half shots of gin
- half a shot of cherry brandy
- half a shot of dry vermouth

**Method**
Shake all the ingredients with cracked ice. Strain and pour.

**Garnish:** cherry

# Rusty Nail

**Glass:** highball

**Ingredients:**
- one and half shots of whiskey (preferably bourbon)
- one and a half shots of Drambuie

**Method**
Mix the ingredients in a bar glass and pour over ice.

**Garnish:** a twist of lemon

**Glass:** cocktail

**Ingredients:**
- one and a half shots of vodka
- one and a half shots of grapefruit juice

**Method**
Frost the rim of the glass with salt. Shake the ingredients with cracked ice. Strain and pour.

**Garnish:** a wedge of lemon

# Salty Dog

# Save the Planet

**Glass:** cocktail

**Ingredients:**
- one shot of vodka
- one shot of melon liqueur (Midori)
- half a shot of blue Curaçao
- a dash of Green Chartreuse

**Method**
Shake the vodka, melon liqueur and blue Curaçao with cracked ice. Strain and pour. Then add the green Chartreuse.

**Garnish:** a cherry

**Glass:** goblet

**Ingredients:**
- two shots of Southern Comfort
- two shots of cranberry juice
- one shot of lime juice

**Method**
Shake all the ingredients with cracked ice. Strain and pour.

**Garnish:** a slice of lime

# Scarlett O'Hara

**Glass:** goblet

**Ingredients:**
- two shots of light rum
- one shot of brandy
- one shot of orange juice
- one shot of lemon juice

**Method**
Shake all the ingredients with cracked ice. Strain and pour.

**Garnish:** an orange twist and a cherry

# Scorpion

# Screwdriver

**Glass:** highball

**Ingredients:**
- two shots of vodka
- two shots of orange juice

**Method**
Pour the ingredients over ice and stir.

**Garnish:** a slice of orange

# Sea Breeze

**Glass:** tumbler

**Ingredients:**
- two shots of vodka
- cranberry juice
- grapefruit juice

**Method**
Pour the vodka over ice. Fill up with equal measures of first cranberry and then grapefruit juice.

**Garnish:** a slice of lime

If this is made as a non-alcoholic cocktail, leaving out the vodka and adding a dash of bitters, and some club soda, it's called a Cat's Paw.

# Sex on the Beach

**Glass:** tumbler

**Ingredients:**
- one shot of vodka
- one shot of peach schnapps
- a dash of lemon juice
- orange juice
- cranberry juice

**Method**
Shake the vodka, peach schnapps and lemon juice with cracked ice. Strain and pour over ice. Top up with equal measures of orange and cranberry juice.

**Garnish:** a wedge of orange

If this is made without the orange juice, it is called a Woo-Woo.

# Side Car

**Glass:** cocktail

**Ingredients:**
- one and a half shots of brandy
- one shot of triple sec
- half a shot of lemon juice

**Method**
Frost the rim of the glass with sugar. Shake all the ingredients with cracked ice. Strain and pour.

**Garnish:** a lemon wheel

# Singapore Sling

**Glass:** highball

**Ingredients:**
- two shots of gin
- one shot of cherry brandy
- half a shot of lemon juice
- a dash of sugar syrup
- club soda

**Method**
Shake the gin, lemon juice and syrup with cracked ice. Strain and pour over ice. Top up with club soda and float the cherry brandy on top.

**Garnish:** a slice of lime

# Sloe Comfortable Screw against the Wall - with a Kiss

**Glass:** tumbler

**Ingredients:**
- one shot of vodka
- half a shot of sloe gin
- half a shot of Southern Comfort
- a dash of Galliano
- a teaspoon of Amaretto
- orange juice

**Method**
Shake the vodka, sloe gin and Southern Comfort with cracked ice. Strain and pour over ice. Top up with orange juice. Then add a dash of Galliano, and float the Amaretto (the kiss) on top.

**Garnish:** a slice of orange, and a twist of orange peel

# Snowball

**Glass:** highball

**Ingredients:**
- two shots of Advocaat
- a dash of lime cordial
- Sprite or 7up

**Method**
Stir the Advocaat and lime cordial together in a bar glass and pour over ice. Top up with Sprite or 7up.

**Garnish:** a slice of lime

An old favorite with cocktail devotees, its low alcohol content allows the Snowball drinker to remain alert while others have long since lost their way.

**Glass:** tumbler

**Ingredients:**
- two shots of Southern Comfort
- two shots of orange juice
- half a shot of pineapple

**for the froth:**
- half a shot of cranberry juice
- half a shot of pineapple juice

**Method**
Pour the ingredients, in this order, over ice. Next shake the cranberry and pineapple juice with cracked ice until a froth is formed, and spoon it over the top.

**Garnish:** a slice of orange

# Southern Frappé

# Stinger

**Glass:** cocktail

**Ingredients:**
- one and a half shots of white Crème de Menthe
- one and a half shots of brandy

**Method**
Shake the ingredients with cracked ice. Strain and pour.

**Garnish:** an orange twist

# Tequila Sunrise

**Glass:** tumbler

**Ingredients:**
- two shots of tequila
- a dash of grenadine
- orange juice

**Method**
Pour the tequila, then the grenadine over ice. Top up with orange juice.

**Garnish:** slices of orange

# Top Banana

**Glass:** tumbler

**Ingredients:**
- one shot of vodka
- one shot of peach schnapps
- two shots of milk
- a third of a banana
- a scoop of cracked ice

**Method**
Mix all the ingredients in a blender until smooth. Pour over ice.

**Garnish:** strawberry, banana and a sprig of mint

Relatively low on alcohol, while very satisfying, this makes a good introduction to alcohol alchemy.

# Venetian Lagoon

**Glass:** goblet

**Ingredients:**
- one shot of blue Curaçao
- one shot of vodka
- a dash of grapefruit juice
- Sprite or 7up

**Method**
First pour the Curaçao, then the vodka. Top up with Sprite or 7up and gently add the grapefruit juice.

**Garnish:** a cherry and a slice of orange

Another cocktail that pleases the eye without making the toes curl.

# Whiskey Sour

**Glass:** highball

**Ingredients:**
- one and half shots of whiskey
- one shot of lemon juice
- one shot of sugar syrup

**Method**
Mix the ingredients in a bar glass and pour over ice.

**Garnish:** a twist of lemon

**Glass:** mug

**Ingredients:**
- one and a half shots of whiskey
- one lump of sugar (or honey)
- one shot of lemon
- four shots of boiling water

**Method**
Put the sugar and the sliced lemon into the mug. Pour a little of the boiling water over them and stir until the sugar dissolves. Add the whiskey and the rest of the water.

**Garnish:** ground nutmeg, a cinnamon stick and cloves (optional)

# Whiskey Toddy

# Zombie

**Glass:** tumbler

**Ingredients:**
- one shot of gold rum
- one shot of white rum
- half a shot of apricot brandy
- half a shot of orange Curaçao
- half a shot of blue Curaçao
- half a shot of grenadine
- a teaspoon of dark, overproof rum

**Method**
Pour everything except the overproof rum over ice, in this order. Float the overproof rum on top.

**Garnish:** slices of orange and a lemon wheel

Without the apricot brandy and blue Curaçao, and with dashes of sugar syrup, lemon and lime juice, this would be a Planter's Punch.

# The Shooters

The art of making a layered shooter consists of delicately pouring the ingredients in a precise order (from the heaviest to the lightest). Pour syrups first, then creams and liqueurs and finally light spirits such as vodka, and fruit juices.

## After Eight

**Glass:** shot

**Ingredients:**
- a third of a shot of Crème de Cacao
- a third of a shot of white Crème de Menthe
- a third of a shot of Bailey's Irish Cream

**Method**
Pour the Crème de Cacao. Next float first the Crème de Menthe, then the Baileys.

## Grandpa is Alive

**Glass:** shot

**Ingredients:**
- a third of a shot of Kahlua
- a third of a shot of Amaretto
- a third of a shot of Absolut vodka

**Method**
Pour the Kahlua. Next float first the Amaretto, then the vodka.

# Jamaican Slammer

# Red, White and Blue

**Glass:** shot

**Ingredients:**
- a third of a shot of triple sec
- a third of a shot of rum
- a third of a shot of Wray and Nephew rum
- five drops of fresh lime juice

**Method**
Pour the triple sec. Next float the rum, then add the lime juice before floating the Wray and Nephew.

**Garnish:** a segment of lime

**Glass:** shot

**Ingredients:**
- a third of a shot of grenadine
- a third of a shot of peach schnapps
- a third of a shot of blue Curaçao

**Method**
Pour the grenadine. Next float first the peach schnapps, then the blue Curaçao.

# Spider Bite

# Thin Blue Line

**Glass:** shot

**Glass:** shot

**Ingredients:**
- one shot of tequila
- a small lime wedge, with twist attached

**Ingredients:**
- half a shot of triple sec
- half a shot of Absolut vodka
- four or five drops of blue Curaçao

**Method**
Pour the tequila and twist the lime over it to release the flavor.

**Method**
Pour the triple sec, and float the vodka over it. Then, with a straw, add the Curaçao drops.